Causeway Coast Way

Game of Thrones® territory

**with Moyle Way
and Rathlin Island**

Eoin Reilly
& Jacquetta Megarry

Rucksack Readers

Causeway Coast Way

Second, fully revised edition published in 2020 by Rucksack Readers
6 Old Church Lane, Edinburgh, EH15 3PX, UK
tel   +44/0 131 661 0262
email   info@rucsacs.com
web   *www.rucsacs.com*

ISBN 978-1-898481-93-5

British Library cataloguing in publication data: a catalogue record for this book is available from the British Library.

Designed in Scotland by Ian Clydesdale (*ian@workhorse.scot*)

Printed and bound in the UK by Short Run Press, Exeter on rainproof, biodegradable paper

FSC
www.fsc.org
MIX
Paper from
responsible sources
FSC® C014540

The mapping in this book was created by Lovell Johns with data from OpenStreetMap.org © OpenStreetMap contributors, CC-by-SA, augmented by original field research by the authors and colleagues (2010-2020)

The name "Game of Thrones" is a Registered Trade Mark owned by Home Box Office Inc of New York, USA.

Publisher's note

All information was checked prior to publication. However, changes are inevitable: take local advice and look out for waymarkers and other signage e.g. for diversions. Walkers are advised to check three websites for updates before setting out:

www.causewaycoastway.com and *www.moyleway.com*
www.rucsacs.com/books/ccw

Parts of these Ways are wet underfoot, and the weather in Antrim is unpredictable year-round. Crossing streams and tidal beaches requires care, especially when in spate and around high tide. The Moyle Way is mainly remote and navigating it requires competence with a compass, especially in mist or low cloud. You are responsible for your own safety, for ensuring that your clothing, food and equipment are suited to your needs and that your intended walk can be safely completed in daylight. The publisher accepts no liability for any ill-health, injury or loss arising directly or indirectly from reading this book.

Feedback is welcome and will be rewarded

All feedback will be followed up, and readers whose comments lead to changes will be entitled to claim a free copy of our next edition upon publication. Please send emails to **info@rucsacs.com**.

Contents

Foreward to the second edition

The Antrim coast offers some of the best walking trails and scenery in Northern Ireland. The Causeway Coast Way and the Moyle Way meet in Ballycastle, and are part of a series of trails that comprise the Ulster Way, which makes a 625-mile (1000-km) circuit of Northern Ireland.

The Moyle Way is 26 miles (42 km) long and it features varied scenery, all of it inland. From Waterfoot it explores the glacial U-shaped valley and iconic waterfalls of Glenariff Forest Park. It then traverses the slopes of Trostan mountain and continues through nature reserves at Slieveanorra and Breen Oakwood before heading north to Ballycastle on the coast.

Ballycastle is the ferry terminus for Rathlin, the only inhabited island in Northern Ireland, and a magnet for wildlife lovers. Its nature reserves are owned by the National Trust and the RSPB, and it is home to Ireland's largest sea-bird colony beside its West Lighthouse. It offers walking of a different kind from the mainland: we describe three routes in detail. Read pages 45 to 50 before deciding whether you want to make a day visit or stay over.

The Causeway Coast Way takes in 32 miles (51 km) of fine coastal walking, with a World Heritage Site, the Giant's Causeway, as its star attraction. Clifftop walks are combined with beach walks, easy promenades and features such as the Carrick-a-Rede rope bridge and Dunluce Castle: see pages 51 to 69.

Walking tourism in Northern Ireland is justly popular, and many more visitors have been drawn to the region in order to visit locations where the fantasy drama series Game of Thrones® was filmed. Although it ended in May 2019, GoT popularity is evergreen. Find out more about these locations on page 25.

Looking east over Fair Head

1 Planning and preparation

This book describes two long routes and island walks. Yourchoices will depend on personal preference, how long you can spare, and how far you have to travel from home. Visitors from a distance could complete all the walks in this book within six days. If you can commit only three walking days, or are inexperienced at long-distance walking, we suggest you try the Causeway Coast Way and visit Rathlin Island. You could postpone the Moyle Way for a return visit.

If you have up to a week and can use a map and compass, however, we recommend you start with the Moyle Way from Waterfoot on the east coast to Ballycastle in the north, follow it with Rathlin as a side-trip and conclude with the Causeway Coast Way from Ballycastle to Portstewart. If you live locally, you could do these on separate trips, returning later for another section, for example over a long weekend.

Some descriptions of Causeway Coast Way and Moyle Way assume that you walk in the opposite direction: see *www.walkNI.com* for example. However, like the operators who offer support services (see page 70), we see the Moyle Way (MW) as a challenging two-day preamble, Rathlin Island as a magnificent interlude, and the Causeway Coast Way (CCW) as the climax of your holiday. Therefore we suggest you make your journey from east to west.

The only downside of this approach it that it places the greatest walking challenge on the first two days. The MW is both more mountainous and more demanding of your ability to navigate. However, it takes you straight to Ballycastle, the ferry port for Rathlin, where you can walk as much or as little as you like, or perhaps hire a bike for a change. The day after requires only a 7-mile walk from Ballycastle to Ballintoy, a gentle day before the culmination of the Giant's Causeway. The final day still holds several surprises and will leave plenty of energy to celebrate on your final night.

If you were to walk in the opposite direction, from Portstewart to Waterfoot, the sequence doesn't work nearly as well. The intensity of the first few days could make the less frequent highlights on the MW feel like an anti-climax. And if you decide the MW is not for you, we still recommend you visit Rathlin first, then walk the CCW from east to west. The Causeway Coast section has the Giant's Causeway as its fitting climax.

Travel planning

Northern Ireland is easily accessible via three airports and two ferry ports. Internal transport offers one regular train service to Portrush and several coastal bus routes. Belfast International Airport has flights from mainland Europe and America, whilst the George Best Belfast City Airport handles flights from airports closer to hand. The City of Derry Airport also has a limited range of services from around the UK and Ireland.

Two main sea ports allow easy access from Scotland and England. P&O sails to Larne from Cairnryan, Troon and Fleetwood. Stena Line sails to Belfast from Stranraer and Norfolk line has sailings there from Liverpool. Consult the public transport map on page 7.

How long will it take?

Refer to Table 1 for distances and suggested stages for the two trails, to which you should add at least one day to visit Rathlin Island. The Moyle Way is the tougher trail, with some difficult terrain and an overall ascent of over 850 m (2800 ft). If you are extremely fit, you could complete it in a single very long day, especially if you shorten it to 21 miles by starting from the road entrance to Glenariff Forest Park. (This option misses the famous waterfalls within the Forest Park.)

If the weather has been extremely wet, consider cutting out the section of trail over Trostan and Slieveanorra, and start your second day from Altarichard Road (relying on a lift from your B&B host or a taxi). You could spend your first day on the short trails within Glenariff Forest Park instead, exploring its fine waterfalls. Resuming the Moyle Way next day, you will have avoided the worst of the waterlogged sections.

Rathlin Island offers many options, including the three trails that we describe on pages 48 to 50. Although most of this is road walking, there is almost no traffic, you could hire a bicycle and in season there's a bus option.

If you are pressed for time, you could shorten the CCW's first day by taking a bus from Ballycastle to Ballintoy. This avoids a long stretch of road walking, along the busy, and mainly vergeless, Whitepark Road (B15). Carrick-a-Rede rope bridge is an easy, and partly offroad, walk from Ballintoy.

The mainline railway reaches the Causeway Coast Way at Portrush, with trains from Coleraine (journey time about 20 minutes on average). Connecting trains take 1½ hours from Belfast or 40 minutes or so from Derry. There are frequent trains on weekdays, with fewer on Sunday.

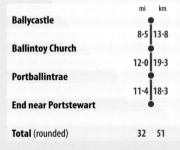

Table 1 Distances and overnight stops

	mi	km		mi	km
			Ballycastle		
				8·5	13·8
Waterfoot			**Ballintoy Church**		
	13·6	21·8		12·0	19·3
Altarichard Rd			**Portballintrae**		
	12·4	19·9		11·4	18·3
Ballycastle			**End near Portstewart**		
Total (rounded)	26	42	**Total** (rounded)	32	51

The main bus service that connects the villages from Ballycastle to Waterfoot is the number 172/402. To reach Ballycastle by bus from Waterfoot would mean changing buses at Ballymena. For bus services that are useful for getting to the start, and away from the finish, of these walks, see below and check online.

Bear in mind that accommodation may also affect your itinerary. Both your budget and preferences, and also the availability at the time you go may affect where you take your overnight breaks: see page 6.

* For historic reasons, Unionists refer to this city as Londonderry, whereas Nationalists call it Derry.

Public transport

Table 2 Selected bus routes

Timetable and journey planner available at *www.translink.co.uk* : check online before relying on this table

bus route	places served	frequency
130	Larne, Ballymena	4 buses daily, except Sunday
131 217	Ballycastle, Ballymena	5 buses daily, except Sunday
140	Portstewart, Portrush, Coleraine	frequent daily service
150	Ballymena, Waterfoot, Cushendall, Cushendun	2 buses daily, except Sunday
171	Ballycastle, Coleraine	2 buses daily, except Sunday
172 402	Ballycastle, Ballintoy, Bushmills, Portballintrae, Portrush, Coleraine	6+ buses daily
218/9	Belfast, Antrim, Ballymena, Coleraine	2 buses daily, except Sunday
234	Coleraine, City of Derry Airport Derry / Londonderry	3 buses daily, 2 Sunday

Lurigethan Mountain (overlooking Cushendall)

Moyle Way

The Moyle Way goes through forestry and across open mountainside. It has several long ascents, two of which push above the 500 m (1640 ft) contour. By contrast, the route of the Causeway Coast Way (CCW) is largely dictated by the coastline and it is always low-lying, albeit in parts it undulates considerably.

Navigating the Moyle Way (MW) is also more challenging than the CCW. Weather will affect your pace: recent rainfall makes for boggy trails and slow progress. In the mountains, gradients will slow you down, as well as terrain. Fog and mist may also hamper your speed, demanding careful navigation on the open hillside. Expect to average up to 3-4 km/hr (2-2·5 mph) when walking the MW excluding stops.

At least one member of your party should be competent at navigating, and it may be prudent to carry GPS as backup: see page 71. Between Waterfoot and Ballycastle, the MW passes through very remote areas. Sections of the trail are poorly signposted and there are some discrepancies with OSNI maps, explained in Part 3. Remain vigilant, keep track of your position on the map and check each junction for signs.

Scramble at western end of White Park Bay

Causeway Coast Way

Navigating the CCW is mostly more straightforward: keep the sea to your right. Signposts are fairly frequent but occasionally a disc, arrow or fingerpost is missing or overgrown. Follow our directions carefully and refer to our mapping whenever in doubt.

The CCW has mixed terrain, with beaches, clifftop paths and some road walking – extensive on day one between Ballycastle and Ballintoy. The route undulates and in places is punctuated by stiles and flights of steps. Overall, you can expect to maintain about 3-4 km/hr (2-2·5 mph) for most of it. You may go slowly over beaches, perhaps while enjoying a barefoot walk or paddle.

White Park Bay has slow going over the rocky scramble at its western end: see photo above. How challenging this is, and whether you can access the beach from the east, depends crucially on the state of the tide. Read carefully the warnings on page 12 and also on page 70.

High winds on clifftop paths may also slow you down. To estimate your day's walking time, allow for rest and refreshment stops, and also for the time you will want to spend visiting castles, watching wildlife and, above all, enjoying the features of the Giant's Causeway.

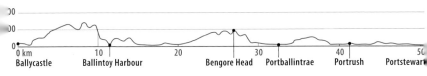

9

What is the best time of year?

Although both trails are open year-round, the months from November through to March are far from ideal. In addition to poorer weather and bogginess underfoot, the hours of daylight are much shorter, fewer buses run and accommodation may be hard to find. The Moyle Way in particular has poor drainage, making its terrain challenging in the wet.

Here are some factors that may affect your decision:

- There is more pressure on accommodation during July and August.
- Biting insects such as midges and horse-flies are most active during summer months, especially July and August. Forested areas on the Moyle Way are the worst afflicted.
- Around the equinoxes (21/22 March and 21/22 September), tides are extra high. This may require careful timing of your walk across White Park Bay: see page 9.
- The Orange Order's marching season peaks on the 12th of July. Although most parades pass without incident, they still affect traffic.
- Bird-watchers may want to visit Rathlin Island between May and July to observe the puffins.
- Some areas along the Moyle Way have shoots during the game season (August to January).

All in all, the ideal time of the year to visit Antrim is from April to June. In spring, more tourist attractions are open, the evenings are getting longer and it is an ideal time for watching wildlife.

Looking west towards Carrick-a-Rede

Experience and preparation

The Causeway Coast Way requires little experience in the way of map-reading, it never ventures above 150 m/500 ft and it's full of points of interest – a good choice for your first long-distance walk. If you are new to such walking, you will enjoy the experience much more if you prepare for it and obtain the proper equipment. Start by getting advice on footwear and waterproofs, for example from our *Notes for novices*: see page 70.

Aim to build up your fitness and ability to navigate before starting out on the trail. Begin with day walks and build up to walking for 4-6 hours at a stretch. If you prefer sociable walking, consider joining a local walking club or go with somebody who has previous experience. If you intend walking independently of a luggage transfer

Beach walking

service, practise carrying extra weight in your rucksack. Unless you are good at travelling light, you may find that such a service helps you to make the most of your holiday.

Route to White Park Bay submerged at high tide

Safety, weather and tides

Heavy periods of rain can cause havoc to sections of the Moyle Way. The banks of the Glenariff River rest on a contained overflow area. If the water level is dangerously high, divert to the Glen Road to the east of the valley. Rain on higher ground can make the going treacherous, although waterproof boots and hiking poles will help. Breathable, windproof and waterproof clothing is essential to keep dry and avoid hypothermia. Your rucksack's contents may become soaked and useless unless protected with a waterproof cover or internal waterproof bags.

Windy conditions also pose risk to walkers, especially on the cliffs of the CCW and Rathlin Island. Beware of leaning into the wind on an unprotected cliff edge: if the wind suddenly drops you may lose balance. Always maintain a safe distance from the cliff edge.

 On the CCW, both ends of White Park Bay may be impassable at high tide. The photo above shows the eastern end with the route line on submerged rocks at high tide. You might have to wait two hours for the sea level to drop enough to keep your feet dry. At the western end, the longer rock scramble (shown on page 9) may be difficult or impossible at tidal extremes, albeit there is an escape route. If the entire beach route is unsafe, the fallback runs along the main road, but that would demand a huge uphill backtrack if you have already descended to the beach. Make your decision before you reach Ballintoy Church: see pages 55-7. Be aware that the sea state, wind and tidal coefficient also affect the window of safety: see page 70 for explanation and for online tidal prediction.

For other reasons, try to avoid high tide for your visit to the Giant's Causeway: at low tide, more basalt columns are exposed and the site is less crowded.

Never rely on a mobile phone in an emergency. There are many 'black spots' at the base of cliffs and in the remote glens of Antrim. For greater safety in remote areas, walk in a group of three so that if an accident occurs, one person can seek help while the third person waits with the casualty.

Responsible walking and dogs

Creating a long-distance trail is a delicate process that requires negotiated access to land. Although large chunks of land are owned by public bodies which are inclined to grant public access where possible, other areas are privately owned and demand that walkers respect the land owner's property and livelihood.

Land in the countryside is the working environment for others. From time to time, operations such as tree felling may mean that diversions are in place. Always follow the instructions on signs posted locally.

Walkers can bring dogs on these trails (except beaches in summer, see below) as long as they keep them on a lead and show proper consideration for wildlife. In areas such as nature reserves, ground-nesting birds must never be disturbed, especially in spring and summer. Dogs on leads can be left attached to tie posts at the Seabird Centre on Rathlin Island: they are not permitted in the centre or on the viewing platform.

Most of the private land across Antrim is used for sheep grazing. Be especially thoughtful before and during the lambing season (any time from January to May). Avoid stress to pregnant ewes and newborn lambs by keeping well away. Give cattle a wide berth, especially those with young.

West from White Park Bay

Code of conduct for walkers

Commercial shooting takes place in the environs of Breen Wood on the Moyle Way between August and January. Keep your dog on a lead lest a sudden loud noise makes it bolt.

Always clean up after your dog if it fouls a footpath. Dogs are prohibited from some beaches from 1 May to 15 September, and from certain sections of beaches year-round, by bye-law of the Borough Council.

Waymarking

Neither Causeway Coast nor Moyle Ways have separate logos, but they are subsets of the Ulster Way: follow its fern leaf logo, sometimes combined with a walker logo. Don't be led astray by signs for the Causeway Coastal Route: it's a 120-mile driving route that sometimes overlaps: see page 71.

Code of conduct for walkers

- ✓ Guard against any risk of fire
- ✓ Leave all farm gates as you find them
- ✓ Keep to the waymarked trail
- ✓ Always use gates and stiles to avoid damage to fences, hedges and walls
- ✓ Take all your litter home
- ✓ Protect wildlife, plants and trees and safeguard water supplies
- ✓ Take heed of warning signs
- ✓ Immediately report any damage caused by your actions to the farmer or landowner
- ✓ Always keep children under close control and supervision, especially on country roads
- ✓ Please do not walk the Ways in large groups, which can be intrusive and noisy

Various signage used on the trails

Accommodation

There is no shortage of accommodation along the Antrim coast,
although advance booking is vital.
The Moyle Way has facilities only at
its ends and for most walkers, 26
miles needs to be split into two days
to be possible, let alone enjoyable.
(However, for the very fit walker in a
hurry, we mention a 21-mile option
on page 6.) To break this walk into
two stages, arrange with a taxi

North Street, Ballycastle

service or B&B owner to collect you from Altarichard Road. Rathlin Island has
very limited options (even in season) and advance booking is essential.

There are several tour operators who can organise your itinerary and make
arrangements: see page 71. Although a package will cost a bit more than
doing it all yourself, your luggage will be transferred while you walk and
there's backup should you run into difficulty.

Those looking for added luxury will find hotels mainly along the north coast
of Antrim, in Ballycastle, Giant's Causeway, Portballintrae, Portrush and
Portstewart. Bed and breakfasts (B&Bs) are found all along the coast on or
near the trail. Many have rooms with private facilities, and most charge
supplements for singles (with or without facilities).

Budget accommodation is plentiful: there are hostels in Ballycastle, Rathlin,
Ballintoy, Bushmills, White Park Bay, Portrush and Portstewart. Camping
barns are found in Glenariff and on Rathlin Island. Official campsites along
either of the walks are sparse: Glenariff Forest Park (MW) and at Glenmore,
outside Ballycastle (CCW). A few caravan parks cater also for hikers, and there
is an informal area for camping on Rathlin Island at Church Bay.

Table 3 Facilities along the Ways

The table shows facilities that existed in 2019. After the 2020 pandemic, some were reopening when we last checked, others were still closed and some may never reopen.

	B&B / hotel	hostel / bunkhouse / barn	campsite	pub/ café	foodshop / takeaway
Cushendall	✓		✓	✓	✓
Waterfoot	✓			✓	✓
Glenariff Forest Park		✓		✓	
Ballycastle	✓	✓		✓	✓
Ballintoy	✓	✓		✓	
White Park Bay	✓	✓		✓	
Giant's Causeway	✓			✓	✓
Bushmills	✓	✓		✓	✓
Portballintrae	✓			✓	✓
White Rocks	✓		✓	✓	
Portrush	✓			✓	✓
Portstewart	✓	✓		✓	✓

What to bring

To enjoy your holiday, travel light. A heavy rucksack can transform your holiday from a pleasure to an endurance test.

Unless you have experience of load-carrying and already know what you can cope with, limit your rucksack weight to a maximum of one-sixth of your body-weight. For most people, this means a top limit of 8-15 kg, and you'll be more comfortable when carrying less. For many people, an easy way to get your rucksack light enough is to use a baggage transfer service and carry only a day rucksack. Even the daysack needs to carry your drinking water, waterproofs, spare clothing, guidebook, camera/phone and (on the MW) food for the day. This will probably amount to at least 4-6 kg.

When booking accommodation, ask if your host can arrange to transfer your luggage to your next lodging. Some B&B owners may be happy to deliver it personally or organise a taxi drop-off. The cost should be less if you are travelling as part of a group. Alternatively, you may wish to pay a tour operator to sort out your logistics, either as part of a group or as a self-guided client.

Camping code

✓ Ask permission before camping in an enclosed field
✓ Camp out of sight of roads, houses and popular areas
✓ Keep groups small
✓ Do not light open fires; handle stoves carefully
✓ Avoid polluting water courses
✓ Bury human waste thoroughly, at least 30 m from paths or water courses
✓ Remove, do not bury, other litter
✓ Leave the site as you found it, or better

Packing checklist

The CCW is well-serviced with easy access to shops. Food and drink supplies can be topped up en route, and water bottles refilled in shops or cafés where you buy something. It's also safe to drink tapwater in your overnight accommodation unless otherwise stated. Most shops and many B&Bs will accept credit and debit cards, but carry cash as backup, especially on Rathlin. There are ATMs in Ballycastle and Portrush.

Grand Causeway

However, the Moyle Way has facilities only at each end, and only two cafés both in Glenariff Forest Park. After that, there are no public buildings on the route, and plenty of sheep on the hills: carry water purifying tablets or a filter, and all the food that you need.

If using a baggage transfer service, a 25-35 litre rucksack should suffice as a daysack, with another bag or suitcase for your main luggage. If carrying everything, you may need a larger rucksack. All rucksacks need an outer waterproof cover. It is easier to pack and retrieve from a roomy rucksack than one that is overfilled. Compression stuff-sacks are very useful for bulky items such as sleeping-bags. If you are staying in hostels, pack a towel, but bed linen should be provided.

Essential

- comfortable, waterproof walking boots
- layers of breathable clothing
- waterproof jacket and over-trousers
- hat (for warmth and sun protection) and gloves
- gaiters (especially for MW)
- compass
- guidebook
- head-torch and whistle
- blister treatment
- sun screen and first aid kit
- toiletries and toilet paper
- enough food and water for each day
- water purification tablets and trowel (for Moyle Way and if camping)
- enough cash in sterling to last to the next cash machine

Desirable

- walking poles (especially for MW)
- light walking shoes or crocs (e.g. for CCW beaches)
- insect repellent and treatment for bites
- small towel (for paddling in the sea or if staying in hostels)
- camera (or smartphone)
- spare batteries and memory cards
- binoculars (for wildlife)
- notebook and pen
- mobile phone (cellphone): useful for arrangements, but never rely on one for emergencies

For campers

The above list assumes that you are using hostels or B&Bs. If you are camping, you'll also need a tent, sleeping gear, cooking utensils, stove, fuel and food, and a much larger rucksack to carry it all.

2·1 The Giant's Causeway

The 'discovery' of the Giant's Causeway was announced to the Royal Society in 1693 amid heated debate about whether it was manmade, natural or created by a giant called Finn McCool: see panel on page 19. Since the end of the 17th century, debate over the Causeway's origins continued worldwide for over a century. Central to the riddle was the question of how basalt was formed.

The original belief was that the stepping stones which emerge from the sea were formed by dead matter being deposited on the ocean floor. Those who supported this argument were known as Neptunists. In 1771 French Geologist, Nicholas Desmarest, put forward the contrary theory that some mountains were in fact extinct volcanoes and that basalt surrounding these areas were volcanic rock. Supporters for this theory were known as the Vulcanists.

When the Scottish geologist, Richard Kirwan, found sea shells embedded in the rocks on Ramore Head in 1799, it seemed to win the argument for the Neptunists. The theory evolved and it is now recognised that the Antrim Plateau was created during the Tertiary/Paleogene period. About 60 million years ago, volcanic activity produced this blanket of basalt. Lava seeped into the crust of the earth producing differing results at the Giant's Causeway and Ramore Head.

At the Giant's Causeway lava collected in a hollow to form a deep pool of molten rock. This large body of liquid retained its heat so that cooling was prolonged,

Lacada Point

Chimney Tops

Port Reostan

Amphitheatre

Roveran Valley Head

The Organ

Port Noffer

Grand Causeway

Shepherd's Path

Port Ganny

Great Stookan

Aird Snout

Portnaboe

Weir's Snout

Low water mark		Cliff edge	

Causeway Coast Way

Other paths

World Heritage Site boundary

Redrawn from original map ©Queen's University Belfast

Visitor Centre

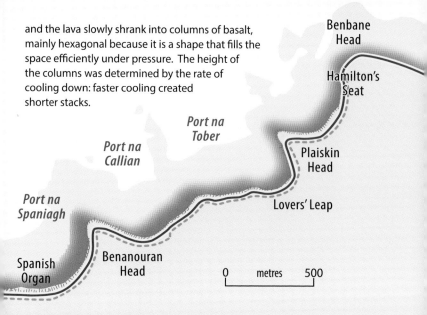

and the lava slowly shrank into columns of basalt, mainly hexagonal because it is a shape that fills the space efficiently under pressure. The height of the columns was determined by the rate of cooling down: faster cooling created shorter stacks.

Several miles away at Ramore Head, this same volcanic activity saw the lava being injected into cracks of sedimentary rock, formed originally on the sea floor. This shale was then baked into a harder rock now known as hornfels.

The hexagonal columns of the Giant's Causeway are not unique: similar formations are found 80 miles away in Scotland (at Fingal's Cave, Staffa) and further afield, in Australia, Germany, India, Patagonia and Vietnam. However, the Giant's Causeway has columns in impressive numbers, and in a grand situation to which people have easy access. In 1986, the UNESCO World Heritage Site citation referred to 'superlative natural phenomena' and 'an outstanding example representing a major stage of earth's history'.

> **The legend of Finn McCool**
>
> *Finn McCool (Fionn mac Cumhail) was a legendary giant who lived on a headland of Antrim. Never having met his rival Benandonner, he rashly challenged the Scottish giant to a fight. Because there were no boats big enough to carry either giant, Finn built a causeway across the sea to Scotland. When Finn saw Benandonner crossing the bridge, he took fright at the size of him and ran home. His wife Oonagh wrapped him in a blanket and he pretended to sleep. Benandonner arrived at the house and demanded to see Finn, and Oonagh said he was coming shortly, but asked him to keep his voice down so as not to wake their baby. Benandonner looked down at the giant 'baby' and ran away in fear of meeting its father. On his way back to his cave in Scotland, he ripped up the causeway behind him.*

Beyond the central causeway area, the UNESCO site extends along 5 km (three miles) of coastline from Benbane Head to Portnaboe. This larger area contains many subtle features which show how repeated volcanic activity has shaped the landscape.

Just above sea level between Port Noffer and Port Ganny are the Grand, Middle and Little Causeways which contain about 38,000 columns in total. Whilst most columns have six sides, many of the hexagons are far from regular, and other columns have anywhere from four to eight sides. Apparently, there is one with only three sides: good luck if you can find it.

The Onion Skin Rock feature lies mid-way between the main Causeway and the Visitor's Centre, at the Windy Gap. It shows the effects of spheroidal weathering: water enters gaps between the columns of stone and expands when it freezes. The rock eventually peels away in layers, like the skin of an onion.

The Chimney Tops are elongated columns in a small cluster which display the durability of basalt. The columns have become isolated while the cliff-face which once surrounded them has gradually eroded away.

Beneath the Chimney Tops is a distinctive band of red rock separating the layers of basalt. During a tropical period, vegetation helped create a soil over the rock. This was then baked by further volcanic activity to create the igneous rock known as *laterite*.

Grand Causeway with Chimney Tops in background

The Giant's Organ is an impressive wall of exposed basalt columns within the cliff face.. Some columns are up to 12 metres tall, with horizontal cracks where tensions in the cooling process created fractures in the rock.

Giant's Organ

Inset:
The Chimney Tops

North over the basalt columns of Grand Causeway

Hamilton's Seat is on top of the cliffs at Benbane Head, named after geologist Reverend William Hamilton. Once a frequent visitor to the Causeway, he carried out a survey of the basalt fields to create a geological map of Antrim in 1786.

Other geology

The white cliffs of Antrim go back further into geological history than the Giant's Causeway. Chalk cliffs, such as those found on Kinbane Head, Larrybane, Ballintoy, White Rocks and Rathlin Island were all originally formed during the Cretaceous period between 65 and 145 million years ago. Skeletons of microscopic organisms called coccoliths built up over time on the ocean floor and became compressed to form chalk. This eventually was pushed up to form part of the mainland, bringing the embedded fossils with it.

The warmer climate of previous eras was interrupted by several Ice Ages over the last two million years. Advancing glaciers from Scotland helped to sculpt the pre-glacial Glens of Antrim. When the last Ice Age ended, about 13,000 years ago, it revealed such features as the classic U-shaped valley of Glenariff. After the massive glaciers, many miles high, finally melted, they released the extreme pressure on the land below, and the land lifted, creating many raised beaches along the Antrim coast. There's a fine example at Ballintoy, where groups of sea stacks now stand beyond reach of the sea.

Elephant Rock at the east of White Park Bay

2·2 History, culture and Game of Thrones®

Dunseverick Castle

With clear views of Scotland from so many places on the Antrim Coast, it is unsurprising that the histories and legends of the two have been entwined.

Little is known of the exact origins of Dalriada, but in the late sixth and early seventh centuries this ancient kingdom included large parts of County Antrim and the west of Scotland. Dunseverick was one of the more prominent castles at the time. Not only was it the central point for the Dalriada in Antrim but it was also on one of the five roads directly linked to the Hill of Tara from where the High Kings of Ireland ruled. It is thought that Dalriada ended when the Vikings arrived in the eighth century.

In terms of historical sites along both the Ways, the next important era was the 16th century. The MacDonnells had arrived from Scotland in the previous century after John Mor MacDonnell married Margery Bisset in 1399. Bisset was heiress to the Glens of Antrim and Rathlin Island. The MacDonnells soon had many rivalries in the area but mainly with the MacQuillans, the O'Neills and the English forces.

Tensions came to a head in 1559 when Sorley Boy MacDonnell landed troops from Scotland to fight the MacQuillans and the O'Neills. The battle was fought at Orra Beg. The MacDonnells covered over large holes in the bog with rushes under the darkness of night. When the O'Neills cavalry charged forward, they sank into these pits and were slaughtered. The battle was won by the MacDonnells as they fought their remaining opponents down the Glenshesk Valley.

Several sites associated with this battle are adjacent to the Moyle Way. The cairn on the top of Trostan was placed there by the MacDonnells. On the slopes of Slieveanorra, there is a tombstone remembering Hugh McPhelim O'Neill. Further along the trail, on the banks of the Glenshesk River is McQuillan's Grave. The main site for the battle, to the east of Orra Beg, is marked on some maps.

The Nine Years War followed shortly after. The O'Neills of Tyrone and O'Donnells of Tyrconnell joined forces against the English in 1594. After the rebellion was quashed, Scottish and English Protestant landlords were given land as part of the Ulster Plantation in 1609. The dispossession of land and continued suppression of Catholics remained a source of unrest over the next four centuries.

Ireland's struggle for independence

Although both parliaments, Irish and British, passed Acts of Union that united the two countries in 1801, resentment of British rule continued. The Irish had been promised Catholic emancipation, but delaying tactics by King George III meant that this did not happen until 1829. By then, it was too little, too late. The demand was now for Home Rule. Later in the 19th century, Liberal governments tried twice, and failed both times, to pass Home Rule legislation. By the beginning of the 20th century, party conflict in Britain had helped to foster strong Protestant unionist feeling in much of Ulster, and made the Irish question yet more complicated.

World War 1 took Irish grievances off the agenda of British politics. Most Irish people were at first supportive of the British war effort, regardless of their political affiliation. Overall, over 130,000 Irishmen volunteered to serve in British forces, and from Antrim alone, over 5000 soldiers died in the conflict. However, as Irish casualties mounted, republican feeling grew in strength, especially in the south of Ireland. In April 1916 there was an insurrection in Dublin – the Easter Rising – in which the rebels used German arms against British soldiers. About 500 people died in this incident, which was swiftly followed by the British execution of its 15 leaders.

This escalated the Irish demand to full independence – a demand vigorously resisted in the north. The formation of the Irish Free State in 1922 brought independence and civil war to the south, which after 1948 adopted 'Republic of Ireland' as its name. From 1922 the six mainly Protestant counties of Ulster remained part of Britain. The Stormont parliament had a built-in unionist majority, which ensured that Catholics continued to be subject to discrimination.

By the 1970s the Catholic minority in Ulster had grown considerably, and Catholic discontent had become less easily ignored. Global awareness of civil rights movements encouraged more militant opposition to anti-Catholic discrimination, which still persisted. This erupted into a period of violence known as 'The Troubles', which lasted some 30 years. Over 3500 people were killed, more than half of them civilians.

In April 1998, the Good Friday Agreement established power-sharing as the basis of a fairer form of devolved government from Stormont. Although deep differences remain within the community, sectarian violence ceased. The peace process has lasted well, and Ulster's natural advantages, including superb scenery and welcoming residents, started to attract visitors in significant numbers.

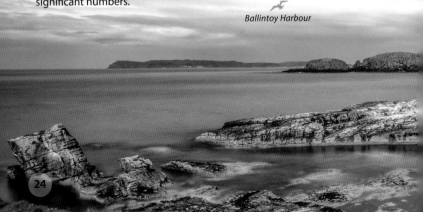

Ballintoy Harbour

The Dark Hedges

Tourism in Ulster received a massive boost from the arrival of the American fantasy series Game of Thrones which ran for eight seasons between 2011 and 2019. This was one of the largest productions in television history, and, out of 14 countries, HBO chose Northern Ireland as its prime location. Production HQ was at the Paint Hall Studios in Belfast where all the interior sets were created. Many scenes were filmed on location in Counties Down and Antrim: see page 71 for a detailed web page and leaflet.

In addition to direct tourism revenue, the GoT factor has boosted Northern Ireland's creative industries and created many jobs in arts and recreation, including themed tours for GoT fans by private car, coach, boat and helicopter. Many scenes were filmed on or near our routes: the lovely valley of Glenariff features as Runestone, and Fair Head (prominent from Ballycastle and beyond) stars as Dragonstone Cliffs.

Offroute, the Dark Hedges consist of majestic beech trees planted in the 18th century on the approach to Gracehill House. The avenue is about 4 miles south of Ballintoy and it was used in GoT as the northern exit of the Kingsroad for escape from the King's Landing.

Portstewart Strand is the long, golden beach that features as the coast of Dorne. Larrybane is to the east of Ballintoy and features as the Stormlands and Nagga's Hill, Old Wyk. Perhaps the most easily recognised location of all is Ballintoy Harbour, which is Lordsport Harbour and Pyke.

Just east of White Rocks, the ruins of Dunluce Castle (see page 65) stand on the clifftop: this was Pyke Castle of House of Greyjoy. (It is also said to have inspired Cair Paravel in C S Lewis' Chronicles of Narnia.) In conclusion, it is pleasing that Ulster, which for over 30 years was infamous for its Troubles, has now become famous for its glorious film locations.

2·3 Habitats and wildlife

Beech fern at a Glenariff waterfall

The two Ways feature strongly contrasting habitats, which support different flora and fauna. The Moyle Way has plenty of forestry and open mountains, whereas Rathlin Island and the Causeway Coast Way feature cliffs and beaches.

Woodland

There are several areas of forest on the Moyle Way with the most diverse at Glenariff Forest Park and Breen Oakwood.

When the waterfalls at Glenariff were developed as a tourist attraction, native broadleaf trees such as oak and beech were planted alongside the rivers. Within the river gorges, rare ferns, mosses and wild flowers now flourish in the soft spray of the waterfalls. The forest park is also a stronghold for the endangered red squirrel. Nut feeders attached to the trees act as magnets and make them easy to spot.

Meadow cranesbill

Red squirrel

Set within coniferous Breen Forest is Breen Oakwood National Nature Reserve – a rare example of mature oakwood. The damp conditions beneath the trees foster a wide range of lichen, mosses and ferns. Red squirrel are here too, and the shy badger. Birds include wood warbler, pied fly-catcher, sparrowhawk, buzzard and (easily spotted) pheasant.

With luck you might see one of Ireland's three species of deer: red deer are native, but sika and fallow were introduced by some of the great landed estates, and there have been many escapees.

Pheasant (male)

Oak leaves at first blush

Fallow deer are rare sightings in the Antrim forests

Upland and wetlands

Large sections of the Moyle Way have poor drainage, acid soil and heavy rainfall. As a result peat forms, covering large areas known as blanket bog. Slieveanorra Nature Reserve shows the importance of blanket bog. You'll see three distinct areas of peat bog in different stages of formation and erosion.

On the lower slopes of Slieveanorra, regeneration pools show how the bog is formed. Bog asphodel, cotton grass and insect-eating sundew and butterwort grow beside these pools. Natural erosion channels can be seen on the main climb up the mountain, with heather and deer grass on the drier ground. At the summit, severe

Red grouse

erosion means the base of the bog reaches the rock underneath.

Wildlife in the vicinity includes red grouse, raven, merlin and hen harrier. You may see Irish hare, especially on Rathlin – an important stronghold for this native mammal, which elsewhere is threatened by the brown hare (*Lepus europaeus*, introduced in the mid-1800s).

Left: Greater butterwort

Below: Irish hare (lepus timidus hibernicus)

Oystercatcher

The Causeway Coast Way is rich in cliff and shoreline walking, with over 80 different types of bird. Birds of prey such as buzzard and peregrine falcon hunt along the cliffs, and smaller song birds such as the skylark and meadow pipit may be seen. Down at the shoreline, waders thrive: look out for oystercatcher and whimbrel.

There is also an abundance of plant life. Along the cliffs you'll see flowers such as kidney vetch, broomrape and sea spleenworth. The coast is also rich in orchids, with frog orchids near the Giant's Causeway and bee orchids along Portstewart Strand.

Bee orchid

Grey seals off Rathlin

Rathlin is a mecca for sea-birds, with its three Nature Reserves and over 100,000 birds. The cliffs and sea stacks near its West Lighthouse host one of the largest seabird colonies in Ireland. The puffin is the main crowd-puller, with other species including fulmar, razorbill, guillemot and kittiwake. Northern Ireland's only breeding pair of red-billed choughs may be seen on its Roonivoolin Trail: see page 48. The island is also home to large numbers of seals, both common and grey: see page 29.

Red-billed chough

Puffin with sand eels

3·1 Waterfoot to Altarichard Road

Distance	13·6 miles 21·8 km
Terrain	riverside path, minor road, boardwalk, forest paths and open moorland which can become extremely boggy in parts
Grade	first 5 miles quite easy, then progressively more difficult with some steep ascents, twice rising above 500 m on rough terrain
Food and drink	Waterfoot; Glenariff Forest Park (Laragh Lodge and visitor centre)
Summary	easy stroll up Glenariff Valley with spectacular scenery, brief steep ascent at waterfalls, forest tracks followed by wild and boggy mountainous stretches with outstanding views

mile 0	5·3		4·3		4·0	13·6
Waterfoot	8·5	**A43**	6·9	**Glendun River**	6·4	**Altarichard Road**

- The Moyle Way starts outside the Mariners Pub on the main street of Waterfoot. It briefly enters a small housing estate for 150 m and exits through a small green area on the right. The path turns left onto the grassy banks of the Glenariff River.

- After 800 m, the trail passes by a wooden bridge over the Altgal Burn: don't cross it, but continue straight ahead. The path steers to the left of the Glenariff River after another 1·6 km (1 mile).

- Follow the course of the Altmore Burn beneath a line of beech trees and cross several stiles.

- After 350 m, the lane meets the Glen Road where you turn right.

The Mariners Pub, Waterfoot

The Glen Road

Ess-na-Crub waterfall

9

▲
Trostan
550

8

7

Ballyemon Road
B14

6

Castlegreen Burn

▲ Slievenanee
543

Ballyeamon ▲
Barn

Essathohan Burn

A43

Glenariff River

Glenariff Forest Pa

Cushendall

A2

Red Bay

A2

Waterfoot

A2

Glenariff River

1

G l e n a r i f f

Glen Road

rockalough 402

A43

2

Altmore Burn

☆
Grey Mare's Tail

3
Callisnagh Bridge

Upper Glenariff Mountain East

Doon Burn

P ☆ Laragh Lodge
Ess-na-Crub

4 ☆
☆
P ☆ **Ess-na-Larach**

P
☆
Visitor Centre

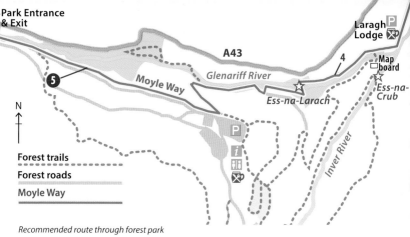

Recommended route through forest park

- At mile 3, the road crosses the Callisnagh Bridge and starts to steepen. Ignore two roads that join from the right and keep ahead.

- Stick to the Glen Road, which undulates before arriving at Laragh Lodge (mile 3·7). Pass to the left of the restaurant and cross the footbridge into Glenariff Forest Park.

- As of 2020, the Moyle Way was not waymarked inside the forest park. We recommend you follow the turquoise route shown above: it climbs steeply in the Glenariff gorge, giving a great view of Ess-na-Larach: see photo opposite.

- At the large map board, first make a short detour by descending the path to its left, soon reaching a viewpoint for Ess-na-Crub and its plunge pool: see photo on page 32.

- Afterwards, return to the map board and take the uphill Waterfalls Trail to its right (red-pecked signage on the ground) for the gorge route. (NB this map board has west at its top, which can be confusing.)

- After 400 m of gorge, you reach a viewing bridge for Ess-na-Larach waterfall. Ignore the first left turn beside a shelter, and keep straight ahead to a T-junction: turn right.

- The gravel path reaches the next junction after 200 m. Ignore the Rainbow Trail signpost to the right.

Upper Glenariff Valley from above the trail

Ess-na-Larach waterfall

- The path rounds some tight bends, then makes a stiff climb of about 400 m to reach a T-junction where you will turn right, just short of the car park. To detour to the Visitor Centre and café (seasonal), head across the car park, then return to the T-junction.

- Pick up the black-marked Scenic Trail which runs parallel to the access road. With views of Glenariff Valley to the right, pass through mature forestry.

- After 800 m you join the access road and follow it for 200 m to the main entrance at mile 5·3. Once this was the official start to the Moyle Way, and many maps show the trail only from this point onwards. The number 150 bus passes the forest park here, connecting Ballymena to Waterfoot.

- Cross the A43 with care and enter an area of felled forestry, as signed. Follow the forestry road upstream beside the Castlegreen Burn. After 1·2 km turn left at a pony trail sign.

- The Way bends around to the right and approaches a ford. If the burn is in spate, you may have to go upstream to cross safely. Within 600 m you meet and cross the Ballyemon Road (B14) at Essathohan Bridge (mile 6·4).

- The track, overgrown in places, climbs beside the forest boundary. After 500 m, pass a small waterfall in the deep river gorge and arrive at an old stone bridge.

- The next section enters dense forestry and signs may be hard to see. Look for a slim break in the

Left turn at mile 6

trees which continues straight ahead for 75 m until it reaches the convergence of two streams.

- Follow the course of the left stream for 400 m. Pass a miniature waterfall before emerging at a 50 m wide fire-break between the trees. Walk carefully across this boggy area to re-enter the forest.

The trail climbs away from the B14

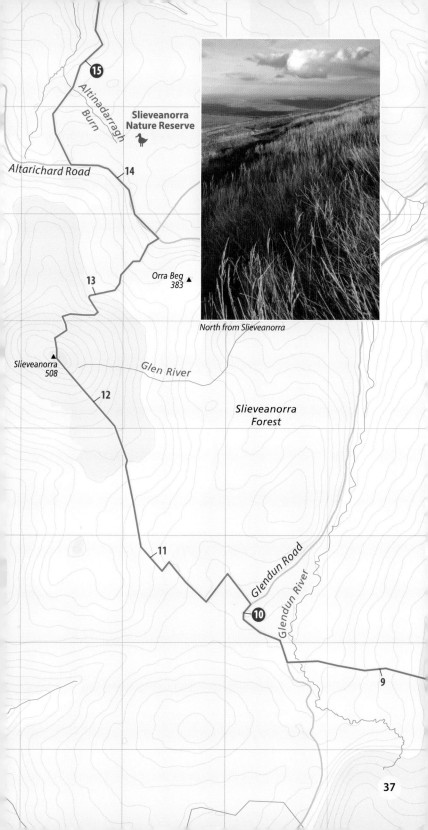

15

Altinadarragh Burn

Slieveanorra Nature Reserve

Altarichard Road   **14**

13

Orra Beg ▲
383

North from Slieveanorra

Slieveanorra
508 ▲

Glen River

12

Slieveanorra
Forest

11

Glendun Road

10

Glendun River

9

- Resume the course of the stream for a further 400 m until you reach two streams. Start by following the stream on the left, and then a raised bank for 200 m, to exit the forest.

- Continue uphill for 300 m alongside the boundary of the forest to the outermost corner. The next section runs across the shoulder of Trostan in a north-westerly direction, sparsely waymarked with posts that may not be intervisible.

- After an initial short climb, the trail enters an area covered with peat hags. After 550 m a small stile crosses a barbed wire fence. This marks the highest point of the Moyle Way (520 m) on Trostan's shoulder.

Stile on Trostan's shoulder

- Over the next 6·5 km (4 miles) the trail had in many places almost disappeared when last surveyed (late 2019). This applies especially to the descent from Trostan and the ascent of Slieveanorra. Careful use of map and compass is needed, especially in poor visibility.

Descending from Slievenorra

- A grassy track now descends down the mountain. After 1·2 km, the trail encounters the source of a river. The terrain gradually gets boggier and there is a river crossing about 400 m downstream.

- The Moyle Way rises a little before crossing a flatter section of bog. It then descends and after 350 m crosses a footbridge over the Glendun River. Rising slightly, the trail continues for 125 m to meet the quiet Glendun Road.

- Follow the road to the right into Slieveanorra Forest. Cross a small bridge and turn left after 800 m onto a gravel forestry road. Cross a stile and continue for 350 m through an avenue of trees. Turn left upon reaching a T-junction.

- Follow a straight road gradually downhill for 550 m. Ignore the first right turn but take the second right onto a 50-m wide channel between the trees leading up the mountain.

- The trail crosses boggy terrain and continues past a large opening on the right, after 550 m. It eventually exits the forest onto the open mountain after a further 500 m.

- The trail enters the Slieveanorra Nature Reserve and continues steadily uphill. It passes a small block of forestry after 650 m and swings more north-westerly. Aim directly at the radio masts of Slieveanorra for the final mile of the ascent.

- Turn right at a tarmac road to cross the summit (508 m/1666 ft). A gravel track begins to weave downhill and enters the forest after 1·2 km.

- The forestry road continues to descend for a further 900 m to meet the Altarichard Road at the foot of Orra Beg. This is the obvious meeting-point for the pre-arranged lift to your accommodation.

3·2 Altarichard Road to Ballycastle

Distance	**12·4 miles 19·9 km**
Terrain	**quiet country roads, forest paths, gravel tracks and an old railway line**
Grade	**overall, a day of descent (over 310 m/1000 ft net loss) with undulations, including a short, steep one at Breen Forest**
Food and drink	**Ballycastle (wide choice)**
Summary	**pleasant forestry paths give way to quiet gravel road at the foot of Agangarrive Hill; cross the boundary of Breen Oakwood and finish the section through Ballycastle Forest Park with great views of Fair Head**

13·6 ○——— 3·5 ———●——— 2·8 ———●——— 2·7 ———●——— 3·4 ———○ 26·0
Altarichard Road   5·6   **Footbridge** 4·5   **Breen Bridge** 4·3 **Ballycastle Forest** 5·5   **Ballycastle**

- After crossing a stone bridge on the Altarichard Road, the road slowly begins to rise. The Way continues for 1·2 km (3/4 mile) and just when an end to the trees comes into sight, the trail turns right, into the forest.

- A forestry track gradually descends for 800 m and crosses a bridge over the Altinadarragh Burn. Ignoring the first right turn, continue to climb gently for 450 m. The gravel road ends abruptly, and a dirt track on the left leads down a fire break.

- The trail briefly dips to cross a stream after 75 m and continues to rise on the far side. It heads away from the water to follow a curve in the trees to the right. The forest floor is firmer here than elsewhere, and after 650 m you reach the edge of the forest.

- Turn left, and descend steeply over the next 400 m through patches of boggy terrain. At the foot of the river gorge, cross a broad concrete bridge over the Altahullin Burn. Climb steeply on a gravel track for 100 m to reach a T-junction where you turn left.

- The gravel road follows the course of the Glenshesk River, sometimes approaching closely, other times at a distance. After 550 m, the route crosses Altaneigh Burn with several large boulders on the left to help your crossing.

Lower slopes of Agangarrive Hill

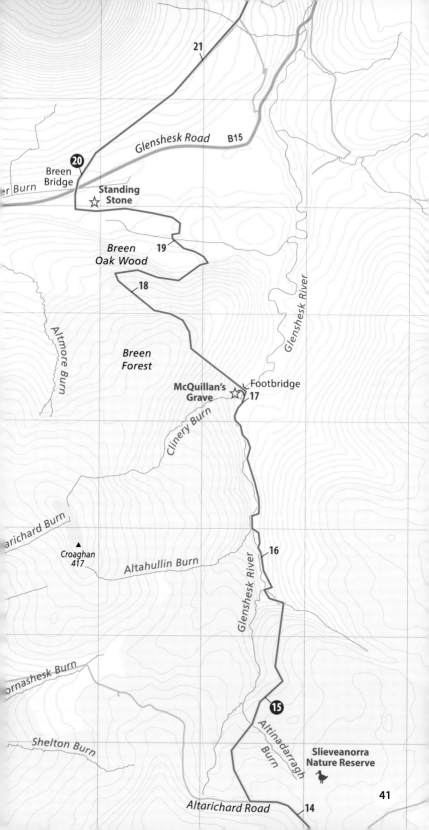

21

Glenshesk Road   B15

20
Breen
Bridge
r Burn
⭐ **Standing
Stone**

*Breen
Oak Wood*   19

18

*Breen
Forest*

Altmore Burn

**McQuillan's
Grave**   ⭐   Footbridge
17

Clinery Burn

Glenshesk River

richard Burn

▲
Croaghan
417   Altahullin Burn

Glenshesk River

16

ornashesk Burn

Shelton Burn

15

Altinadarragh
Burn

**Slieveanorra
Nature Reserve**
🐦

41

Altarichard Road   14

- A further 1·2 km down the road, the trail passes the ruin of a shepherd's cottage. After 200 m a sign points to MacQuillan's Grave. If the river is too deep to cross here, you can reach it from 250 m further down the river where the trail crosses a footbridge.

McQuillan's Grave

- The trail follows the boundary of Breen Forest until it reaches a larger block of forestry near the ridge-line. The ascent is steep, climbing 120 m over a distance of 600 m. The Way then turns left and follows the bank of a ditch for 100 m to meet the main forestry road.

- Turn right and follow the road as it rises gently to round the shoulder of Bohilbreaga at a height of 285 m (935 ft). On the descent, the forest opens up on the right, giving views over Knocklayd, Rathlin Island and Fair Head.

- The trail continues downhill and passes a turn-off for the 'Breen Forest Way' after 900 m, soon rounding a hairpin bend. You are looking across felled forestry into Breen Oakwood. After 530 m, enter a forest of mature conifers.

- The descent steepens and after 400 m you arrive at a T-junction: turn left. This leads to an area of mixed deciduous trees amongst the oakwood.

- Soon you pass a small quarry with a pond before reaching a hairpin bend at the bottom of a hollow. The trail leaves the wooded area to continue along a lane lined with hawthorn.

- After 800 m you reach the entrance barrier to Breen Oakwood. Continue past a farm settlement and round a sharp bend to the right to reach the main road.

- Cross the main road and ascend Drumavoley Road along the flank of Knocklayd for the next 4·4 km (2¾ miles). The tarmac road rises and falls continuously before arriving at a left turn into Ballycastle Forest.

Crossing the Glenshesk River to Breen Forest

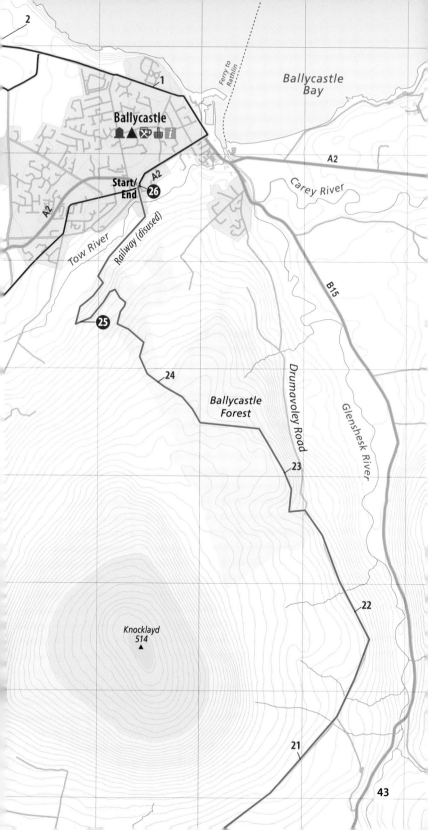

Ballycastle Bay

1

Ferry to Rathlin

Ballycastle

🏠▲✂️🏢ℹ️

A2

Start/ End 26

A2

Carey River

Tow River

Railway (disused)

B15

25

24

Drumavoley Road

Ballycastle Forest

Glenshesk River

23

22

Knocklayd
514
▲

21

- After the end of the car park, take the first turn right. The trail climbs steadily past two large hollows on the left, reaching a Y-junction after 650 m. Bear left and continue to ascend.
- The next junction is within 175 m: turn sharp left uphill. Pass straight through a small crossroads after 100 m. The trail levels off, with views of Rathlin Island and Fair Head.
- Reach a T-junction after a further 450 m and turn right. The summit of Knocklayd starts to appear above the trees. The trail crosses the shoulder of the mountain at a height of 210 m (690 ft), and begins to descend.
- The surface of the trail soon changes from tarmac road to gravel. After 425 m, the Way continues past a right turn. The descent steepens and the trail passes by a second right turn after 450 m. After a further 725 m, enter a copse of silver birch and at the next T-junction, turn left.
- This narrow path steadily descends to a sharp left bend and reaches another hairpin bend after 700 m. The trail double-backs from the edge of the forest and continues on more level terrain. After a further 600 m, you join the path of an old narrow-gauge railway: see panel below.
- After 700 m pass beneath an old bridge and turn left. Follow a quiet street for 300 m to the centre of Ballycastle. The Diamond marks the end of the Moyle Way and the beginning of the Causeway Coast Way: see pages 51 and 53 (map).

> **Antrim railways**
>
> *Work began on the Ballymoney to Ballycastle narrow-gauge line in 1878, and within two years the 16 miles of track was complete. Several companies were opening competing lines about then. In 1924, the Northern Counties Committee bought the failing Ballycastle line for £12,500.*
>
> *With internal trouble in the 1920s and the onslaught of World War 2, large sections of railway line had become damaged and many train companies were on the verge of bankruptcy. To keep the country moving, the 1947 Transport Act nationalised the railways.*
>
> *The Ballymoney to Ballycastle line was one of many casualties in Antrim, closed down by the Government within three years. Today, many relics from this period lie scattered about the country, such as this bridge near Ballycastle.*

Bridge over the old Ballycastle railway line

4 4 Rathlin Island

These three walks on Rathlin total over 18½ miles, each exploring a different corner of the L-shaped island, which has fine views of Kintyre (Scotland) and Antrim. Roads make up over 80% of these trails, but fortunately traffic is sparse. Visit the Rathlin Boathouse Visitor Centre on arrival: it's normally open from Easter to September: tel 02820 760 064.

> **Ferries from Ballycastle**
> Two ferries serve Rathlin Island from Ballycastle year-round, weather permitting, booking essential. The fast ferry carries only passengers and takes 25 minutes, whilst the car ferry takes 45 minutes. Before the pandemic, sailings were frequent but after lockdown in mid-2020 they were twice daily at much-reduced capacity. The adult return fare was £12 in 2020. For the current timetable and booking procedure, tel 02820 769 299 or see www.rathlinballycastleferry.com.

If you can make only a day trip, book the first ferry out from Ballycastle and the last one back: see panel above. Even so, choose between Walk 1 and Walk 3 (pages 48 and 50), because there won't be time to do both unless you hire a bike from the Soerneog View Hostel (must be booked: see page 71). If your visit is between May and July and you want to see Rathlin's famous puffins, don't miss Walk 3 with its huge cliff colonies of sea-birds. If scenery, seals and off-road walking are more important, you may prefer Walk 1. Walk 2 is short enough to combine with either.

You can also enjoy the puffins in season without walking: two private bus operators normally meet incoming ferries to take visitors to the RSPB site.

Staying overnight makes for a more relaxed visit and lets you split your walking over two days. Given the island's small population (about 150), the options are limited. In 2019 three B&Bs, two hostels, four glamping pods and a bunkhouse were open in season, but after the pandemic in 2020 the island closed down for over three months. Post-lockdown provision has yet to emerge, but advance booking is essential at all times. See page 71 for Rathlin websites and pages 46-7 for a map.

Options for food and drink on Rathlin are limited. All are centred on the harbour, five minutes walk from the ferry. There's one pub, usually open year-round. In season only, the Manor House serves food and drink, and there may be an informal tea room and chip van.

Boat in front of the old pier, Church Bay

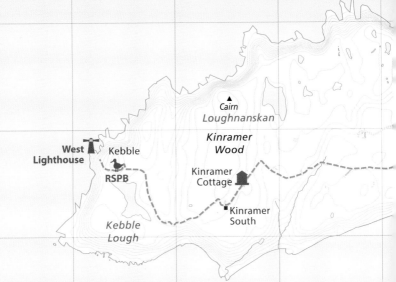

Rathlin tourism is mainly driven by its nature reserves. The Royal Society for the Protection of Birds (RSPB) owns two sites: Kebble Nature Reserve boasts one of Ireland's largest sea-bird colonies and Roonivoolin allows public access to a breath-taking cliff walk. The National Trust own a third nature reserve which preserves the Crocknanagh traditional field system and celebrates the island's farming history: see page 49.

The human history of the island is as fascinating as its wildlife. Inhabited for nearly 8000 years, Rathlin's dramatic past stretches from the invasion of the Vikings to several massacres by English forces that wiped out the MacDonnell Clan in the 16th century. Its dramatic coastline is marked out by three lighthouses to warn shipping of the rugged cliffs and underwater hazards. Still, over 40 recorded shipwrecks lie in the wild waters offshore.

Approaching Rathlin Harbour

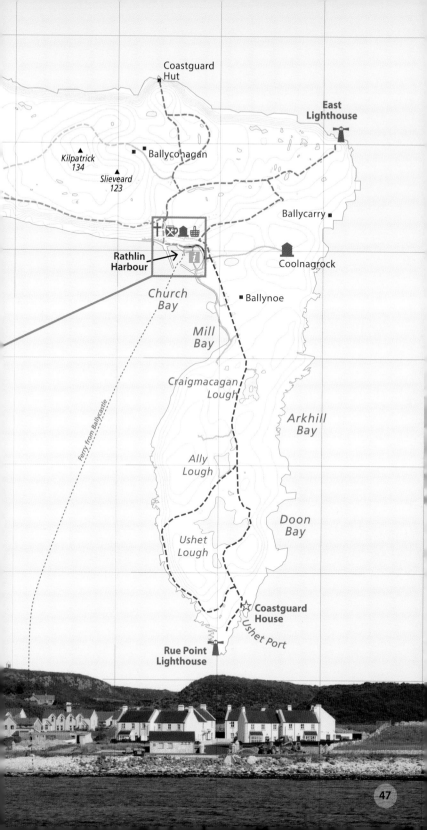

Coastguard
Hut

East
Lighthouse

Kilpatrick
134

Slieveard
123

Ballyconagan

Ballycarry

Coolnagrock

Rathlin
Harbour

Church
Bay

Ballynoe

Mill
Bay

Craigmacagan
Lough

Arkhill
Bay

Ferry from Ballycastle

Ally
Lough

Doon
Bay

Ushet
Lough

Coastguard
House

Ushet Port

Rue Point
Lighthouse

Walk 1: The South Lighthouse and Roonivoolin Trail

Distance (round trip): 10 km (6 miles)

- From the ferry, turn right and follow the curve of the harbour for 550 m all the way round to the old pier. Stick to the coastline to pass (or visit) the Boat House (visitor centre) with its plaque to Robert the Bruce.

- Just after the glamping pods, turn left to pass Rathlin Hostel, then right at the road.

- Follow the undulating tarmac road for 1·6 km (1 mile). On an uphill stretch soon after a reed-fringed loughan, look for a gate on the right (signed Roonivoolin Trail) leading down beside Ally Lough.

- The trail gradually rises, threading its way through two hillocks to reach the cliffs within 850 m. Cross the stile and turn left to follow the cliff-top path (exposed in places).

- After 900 m of glorious views, at a field corner climb two stiles to head back inland (avoiding the private land of Rathlin's southern tip). Follow the fence north-east to reach a gate onto the road after 400 m.

- Turn right down a steep hill for 200 m to reach the shore at Ushet Port, beside the Coastguard House.

i The Coastguard House

Ushet Port was once the main landing point for boats. Rathlin's southern tip was the closest point to Ballycastle on the mainland. Tobacco and alcohol were smuggled in and hidden behind the false walls of the Coastguard House.

When the Water Guards arrived on Rathlin in the early 19th century, they filled in the natural harbour at Ushet Port with boulders (now used by seals) and built a Coastguard House here. They helped to develop the main harbour area at Church Bay, where their former boat house now acts as a visitor centre.

- A narrow track continues for another 400 m to the South Lighthouse. Look closely at the rocks: some may arch their backs and identify as seals!

- Return by retracing your steps to the harbour.

South Lighthouse and Rathlin's rugged coastline

Walk 2: The East Lighthouse and Ballyconagan Trail

Distance (round trip): 7·5 km (4·5 miles)

- From the ferry, turn right and walk 350 m to McCuaig's Bar. Turn left up the street beside the pub, then turn left at the crossroads.

- Continue uphill for 200 m, then turn right. The road undulates, mainly climbing, to reach a T-junction after 900 m.

- Turn right on a gravel road for 750 m to reach the gates of the East Lighthouse. To the right are cubes of concrete marked "Lloyd's"– remains of foundations for Marconi's radio aerial: see panel and page 51.

- Return to the T-junction, but go straight over. After 850 m turn right down an unmarked lane. (A black National Trust sign is just visible from the junction.)

- After 150 m, turn right at the white NT sign and climb the stile for the Ballyconagan Trail (also called the Crocknanagh Trail). Turn left at the first junction, marked by a post with a white disc. After 450 m, the trail bears left.

- After a further 350 m through the heather, enter the old Coastguard Hut with views to Islay, Jura, Kintyre and Arran identified by a location finder.

- Return to the previous junction and turn left to follow the waymarked loop trail which takes in the remains of the Crocknanagh settlement which dates from the 1830s. This returns you the lane after 900 m. When you reach the road, turn right.

- Walk 350 m to a junction at a church and turn left. Go downhill towards the harbour for 200 m and turn left to return to the ferry terminal.

East Lighthouse with Kintyre in the distance

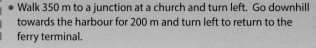

> **Marconi**
>
> In 1898 Guglielmo Marconi was commissioned to develop a wireless system to send news of transatlantic ships at sea. The insurers, Lloyds of London, needed to know of their safe return.
>
> Rathlin Island was considered the end point of the dangerous Atlantic crossing before onward passage to ports such as Belfast, Glasgow and Liverpool. Marconi created two bases – Ballycastle and the East Lighthouse on Rathlin. His first successful radio transmission between these points was on 6 July 1898.

Walk 3: The West Lighthouse

Distance (round trip): 13 km (8 miles)

- If your time is tight, be aware of the option to use a bus (in season). From the ferry, turn left towards St Thomas's Church. After 200 m, turn right up a steep hill for a further 200 m to a T-Junction.

- Turn left and follow the road as it sweeps around to the left past another church. Continue up the hill, past a memorial to those who emigrated during the Famine.

- Follow the undulating road for 5 km (3 miles), gradually climbing overall. You pass the edge of Rathlin's only forest, Kinramer Wood.

- The road peaks at just over 100 m (330 ft), crossing a cattle grid into Kebble Nature Reserve.   The final 1·1 km is on a rocky road which dips towards Kebble Lough before rising around cliffs to the West Lighthouse and RSPB viewing platform.

- From here, retrace your steps all the way back to the harbour.

Cliffs of the RSPB reserve with nesting fulmars in foreground

5·1 Ballycastle to Ballintoy Church

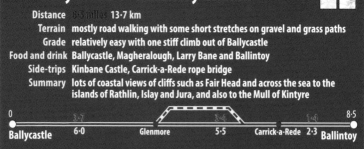

Distance	8·5 miles 13·7 km
Terrain	mostly road walking with some short stretches on gravel and grass paths
Grade	relatively easy with one stiff climb out of Ballycastle
Food and drink	Ballycastle, Magheralough, Larry Bane and Ballintoy
Side-trips	Kinbane Castle, Carrick-a-Rede rope bridge
Summary	lots of coastal views of cliffs such as Fair Head and across the sea to the islands of Rathlin, Islay and Jura, and also to the Mull of Kintyre

```
0          3·7                    3·4              1·4      8·5
Ballycastle  6·0      Glenmore        5·5   Carrick-a-Rede  2·3  Ballintoy
```

The Causeway Coast Way officially starts from the Diamond: see map on page 53. If you have just returned from Rathlin Island, skip to the next bullet. Follow Ann Street, then Quay Road north-east for 850 m from the Diamond to reach the harbour. Turn left uphill on the pavement of North Street, soon passing the ferry terminal to Rathlin.

After 350 m, you pass a small green on the right with a boulder memorial to Guglielmo Marconi, pioneer of radio transmission: see panel on page 49. The route starts a steady climb, rising 50 m over the first 1·2 km (0·8 mile).

The road bends left and continues uphill for 800 m (now as Clare Road) to pass the Causeway Coast Holiday Park on the right. After a further 400 m pass Hayes caravan park on the left. (Moyle Road, a possible shortcut from the Diamond, joins here: see page 53.)

Just after Atlantic View Leisure park, Clare Road makes a sharp left turn, but you leave it to go straight ahead on a track between two fields.

After the track rises to meet a small housing estate, turn left to follow a road through the Carnduff estate.   Within 170 m you meet the main Whitepark Road (B15): turn right.

The Diamond, Ballycastle

- The road heads inland, and at mile 2·9 reaches a right turn signed 'Kinbane Head'. This 3 km (2 mile) detour descends steeply to the car park and walkway to Kinbane Castle: see panel below.

- Otherwise, follow the straight road gently uphill. At mile 3·7, it bends right past Glenmore campsite. Should you prefer to escape the busy traffic of the B15 you could bear left instead, to follow the narrow, quiet Glenstaghey Road. It rejoins the B15 at mile 5·7.

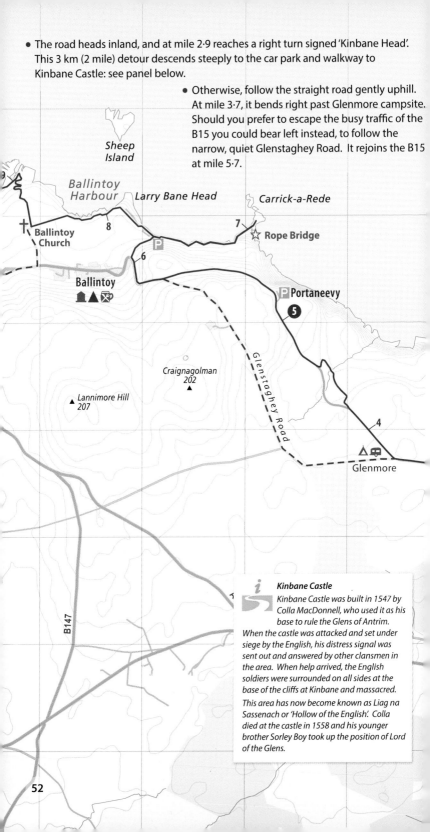

Sheep Island

Ballintoy Harbour

Larry Bane Head

Carrick-a-Rede

7

☆ Rope Bridge

8

✝ Ballintoy Church

6

P

P Portaneevy

5

Ballintoy

Glenstaghey Road

Craignagolman
202
▲

▲ Lannimore Hill
207

4

△ Glenmore

B147

Kinbane Castle

Kinbane Castle was built in 1547 by Colla MacDonnell, who used it as his base to rule the Glens of Antrim.

When the castle was attacked and set under siege by the English, his distress signal was sent out and answered by other clansmen in the area. When help arrived, the English soldiers were surrounded on all sides at the base of the cliffs at Kinbane and massacred.

This area has now become known as Liag na Sassenach or 'Hollow of the English'. Colla died at the castle in 1558 and his younger brother Sorley Boy took up the position of Lord of the Glens.

52

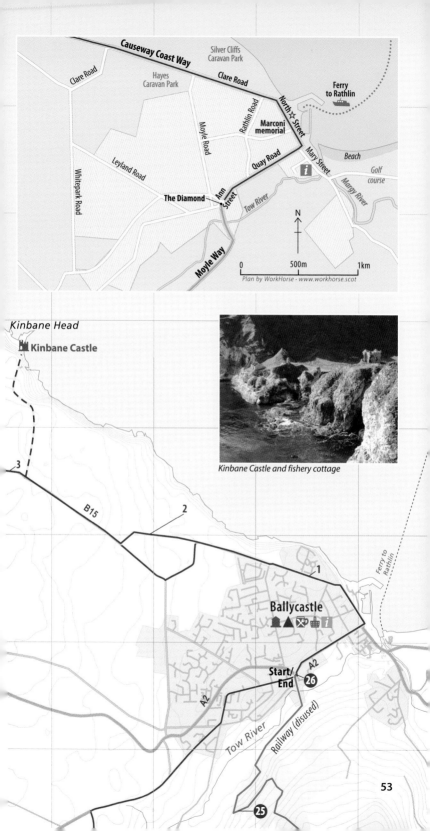

Causeway Coast Way

Clare Road

Silver Cliffs
Caravan Park

Hayes
Caravan Park

Clare Road

North Street

Ferry
to Rathlin

Moyle Road

Rathlin Road

Marconi
memorial

Leyland Road

Quay Road

Mary Street

Beach

Golf
course

Margy River

Whitepark Road

The Diamond

Ann Street

Tow River

ℹ

N

0   500m   1km

Plan by WorkHorse · www.workhorse.scot

Moyle Way

Kinbane Head

🏰 **Kinbane Castle**

3

B15

2

Kinbane Castle and fishery cottage

1

Ferry to Rathlin

Ballycastle
🏰 ▲ ⊠ 🏛 ℹ

Start/
End **26**

A2

A2

Tow River

Railway (disused)

25

- Otherwise, stick to the B15 for a further 650 m. Where it bends left, signed for Bushmills and Ballintoy, leave it to go straight ahead downhill on the minor road.

- This quiet road meanders through a hollow with a farmstead and climbs up again. After 700 m, turn right to rejoin Whitepark Road (the B15).

ℹ Carrick-a-Rede rope bridge

*This rope bridge was strung each year by salmon fishermen to span the 30-metre chasm joining Carrick Island to the mainland. It allowed them to get their nets in the best place, and to get their catch from sea on to ice within 12 minutes. Now cared for by the National Trust, it is normally open year-round, weather permitting, with admission by timed slot booked online. In 2020, adult admission cost £10 but the bridge was closed. Visit **nationaltrust.org.uk** for details.*

- The B15 approaches the coast again and within 750 m reaches Portaneevey car park. Divert briefly to enjoy its viewpoint with location finder: you'll see Sheep Island ahead, Carrick-a-Rede rope bridge below and Rathlin Island to the right.

- Continuing on the Way, the road veers west and starts to descend. Just after the Glenstaghey Road rejoins (mile 5·7), it bends right, and you can spot the distinctive whitewashed church of Ballintoy distant to the right.

- After a further 250 m at a sharp left road bend, turn right (mile 6·1) for the access road to Carrick-a-Rede and Larry Bane. Descend for 300 m to reach a roundabout at the car park.

- Turning left would send you on the Way towards Ballintoy Church, but most walkers will turn right to visit the exciting rope bridge, which adds an extra 2·2 km (1·4 miles) return: see panel.

- The Weighbridge Tearoom is on the left, with toilets. If the bridge is closed, a notice at the the pay-point ahead will say so, but you can still pass through to explore the site and approach the bridge closely (free of charge).

- After the bridge, return to the car park. If you are staying in Ballintoy, return to the main road, turn right and reach the village within 500 m.

- To continue the Way, head west by bearing left on a narrow path along the top of a disused chalk quarry at Larry Bane. The fingerpost says 'Ballintoy Harbour 3·5 km' but does not mention the CCW. Cross some fields with views to Sheep Island, Rathlin and Kintyre beyond.

- About 1·3 km after the car park, the Way emerges to meet Harbour Road at Ballintoy Church (mile 8·5). Turn left here for the road bypass to avoid White Park Bay tidal difficulties: see page 55. Turn right to continue the Way.

Carrick-a-Rede rope bridge and salmon fishery cottage

Distance	12·0 miles 19·3 km
Terrain	mainly gravel and grass cliff top paths with sections of sandy beaches with some rocky scrambling and a few short road links
Grade	varied gradients with undulations & flights of steps
Food and drink	Ballintoy Harbour, Portballintrae
Side-trips	Giant's Causeway Visitor Centre, Bushmills Distillery
Summary	a fine sequence of coastal scenery packed with many points of interest, culminating with the Grand Causeway

8·5   2·9   1·7   4·6   2·8   20·5

Ballintoy 4·7 **Portbraddan** 2·7 **Dunseverick Castle** 7·4 **Giant's Causeway VC** 4·5 **Portballintrae**

 Before committing yourself to White Park Bay, check tide times: see page 70. The headland at the eastern end of the bay is often impassable around high tide. Also the rocky scramble at the western end can become very challenging – but there is an escape route. To bypass the beach route, turn left up Harbour Road, turn right along the main road for 4 km and turn right down Portbraddan Road to resume the Way: see map on page 57.

Otherwise, turn right down Harbour Road past Ballintoy Church, and follow it as it zigzags steeply down to the sea. After 850 m, it arrives at Ballintoy harbour, a famous location to GoT fans.

Notice a lime kiln on the left, and information boards about the white limestone, sea birds and GoT filming: see page 25. Follow the shoreline path, well-defined at first, through gates/stiles across the raised beach. Enjoy fine views of sea stacks, arches and the wonderful Elephant Rock: see page 22.

 Just beyond Elephant Rock comes the headland shown on page 12. If the sea state and your agility make it safe to proceed, go around it with care: the rocks can be very slippery, but any difficulties are brief. Just around the headland lie the glorious sands of White Park Bay.

Cross the 2·5 km (1½ miles) of superb beach to pass under Portbraddan cliffs. At the beach end, there's a stiff scramble over the rocks – if it's safe to proceed. (If not, backtrack to escape by the uphill path before the cliffs.)

Ballintoy Church

Across the bay to Geeragh Point

- Go up towards the houses and turn right in front of them. (The road bypass route rejoins the Way here.)
- After Portbraddan Cottage (NT) take a narrow path at the base of the cliffs. After 300 m, it rises to pass through the hole in an old sea arch at Gid Point.
- Descend the slippery rock steps with care and cross a rocky beach by two ladder stiles. Head inland on an intricate section across farmland, carefully following signs around field edges, over stiles and across footbridges.

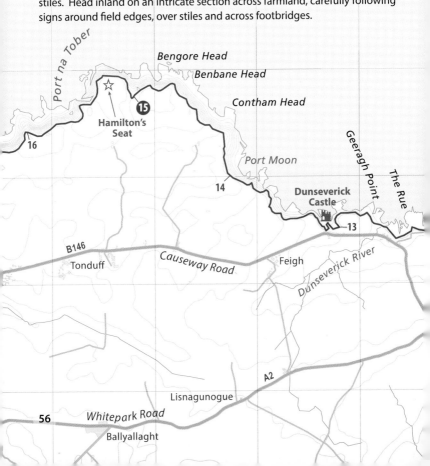

Ruins of Dunseverick Castle

- At about mile 12·1, the trail forks right to descend to the shoreline, crossing a field to reach Dunseverick car park with toilets and slipway.

- Follow the road uphill for 150 m and turn right to descend into a field by stone steps. The trod path then turns left (no waymarker) and rises before halting abruptly at a cliff drop with fine views across the bay.

- Turn left to pass around the bay, crossing first a small footbridge, then a larger one over a river which cascades down the rock-face into the sea.

- Continue along a grassy path around Geeragh Point, after which you start to see Dunseverick Castle on the promontory to your right. Turn right just before the road and enter a car park; the castle information board (over the wall) was in 2020 too faded to read.

- The trail follows a grassy clifftop path fenced off from the fields to the left. Gaps in the dense vegetation allow intermittent fine coastal views in both directions.

Horse Shoe Harbour with Nurse and Child at upper right

- The path continues for about 850 m to reach a small headland with views over the promontory of Benadanir. Just beyond, at Port Moon, the remains of an old salmon fishery cottage sit at the base of the cliffs.

- The trail ascends over a further 850 m to reach Contham Head (mile 14·4). Later, at mile 14·7 it crosses a stile to arrive at Bengore Head, the highest point of this section with cliffs over 100 m high. Look behind you for views all the way east to Fair Head.

- The trail undulates further over the next 1 km and enters the UNESCO World Heritage Site at Benbane Head (mile 15·3): see the map on pages 18-19.

- The trail swings left and as you round the corner, you glimpse distant mountains ahead: these are in Donegal, in the Republic. Further on, look back down over Horse Shoe Harbour, a rocky outcrop with two basalt columns affectionately known as the Nurse and Child: see photo above.

- The trail makes steep undulations over Plaiskin Head and Benanouran Head (mile 15·7).
- From the headland, look over to the reef off Lacada Point. An information board explains about the sinking of La Girona: see panel.
- Just beyond the next headland are the Chimney Tops, leading to the bay backed by the Amphitheatre. At its far end, visit the viewpoint to your right, Roveran Valley Head: you'll probably see tiny-looking people on the paths far below.
- At mile 16·8, turn right to descend the steep flight of steps on the Shepherd's Path. (The path ahead also leads to the Visitor's Centre, but runs inland among vegetation and misses good views of the finest of the Causeway's features.)
- Descend all 162 steps and walk down a path to reach a T-junction within 250 m. It's worth making a 400-m detour to the right. This path passes under the Giant's Organ (see page 21) and gives views of the Amphitheatre with Chimney Tops and Giant's Harp around the corner.

North-west from the Amphitheatre

i La Girona
The Spanish Armada set out to overthrow Queen Elizabeth I in 1588. Retreating after their initial attack, the fleet of ships sailed around the top of Scotland and Ireland to get back to Spain. Along the northern and western coasts, the Armada encountered severe storms which destroyed over 20 vessels.

Already carrying 800 survivors from two other shipwrecks, the heavily laden La Girona crashed into the reef. Only five of the 1300 people on board survived. For several weeks dead bodies were washed up on the shores. Some of these are said to be buried in St. Cuthbert's Graveyard, across the road from Dunluce Castle.

Sea Gull Isle, Port Noffer

- Return to the T-junction and keep straight on downhill to Port Noffer. After 350 m, a side-path on the right leads to the Giant's Boot: see below.

- A further 150 m of path leads to the focal point of the Grand Causeway on the right, flanked by Middle and Little Causeways to its left.

- The trail continues on around the bay of Port Ganny. The road begins to rise over the first 500 m through the Windy Gap. Once through the gap, the road continues a steady climb for a further 500 m to reach the Visitor's Centre: see panel.

- Walk west from the Visitor Centre up a stepped path that passes behind the Causeway Hotel and continues towards Runkerry Point at mile 18·5.

i **Giant's Causeway Visitor Centre**
The National Trust has cared for the Giant's Causeway since 1961. Its role is to conserve the landscape and educate the public on the heritage.
In 1986 it became a UNESCO World Heritage Site and visitor numbers have increased ever since.
The current Visitor Centre cost over £18 million, opened in 2012 and combines striking architecture with energy saving and water conservation. It offers audio guides in 11 languages, café, shop and exhibition with a video of the Finn McCool legend.
After the 2020 pandemic, the centre reopened with visitor numbers controlled by timed slots pre-booked online at **nationaltrust.org.uk/giantscauseway** *tel: 02820 731 855.*

The Giant's Boot

Basalt columns

Giant's Causeway World Heritage Site

Lacada
Point

Amphitheatre

The
Organ

Port Noffer

Grand Causeway

Port
Ganny

Great Stookan

Portcoon

Runkerry Point

16

17

18

Aird

Ardihannon

Visitor Centre

Carnside

Causeway
Head

19

Runkerry Beach

Giants Causeway and Bushmills Railway

Bush River

Port Ballintrae

P

20

Portballintrae

21

B145

A2

A2

Gortnacapple

Bushmills

Bushmills

Bushmills – Giant's Causeway steam train

- If time permits, consider a side-trip on the steam train to Bushmills, to visit the world's oldest distillery: see panel.

- The Way passes along the clifftop with fine views of Great Stookan to your right. At the first headland a sign announces the end of the World Heritage site.

- At mile 18·2, look down over the dramatic inlet of Portcoon. After a flight of timber steps, pass a memorial to two pilots whose training flight in 1942 crashed nearby.

> **i** **Bushmills Distillery**
>
> *Bushmills is the world's oldest licensed distillery. Its licence dates from 1608, although the distilling in this area goes back several centuries further. Irish emigrants helped to establish a market for Bushmills in the United States prior to Prohibition (1920-33). After the ban was lifted, large stockpiles of Bushmills Whiskey were ready for export, increasing its market share.*
>
> *A narrow-gauge line connects the Giant's Causeway to the village of Bushmills. A steam train makes several return journeys each day along the 3 km of restored railway line. Distillery visits take about 40 minutes; cost in 2020 was £8. For opening times and restrictions, see **www.bushmills.com**.*

- Rounding the next headland, you pass the Victorian grand mansion of Runkerry House on your left (now luxury apartments). Go ahead past the slipway on the right to reach the ruins of Blackrock fishery station.

North-east toward Runkerry House

- About mile 19, a small wooden bridge crosses Runkerry Burn at the start of Runkerry beach. The Way climbs a sand dune and continues uphill to meet the train line. (You could turn right if you prefer to walk across the beach, turning left at its far end for the bridge.)

- The Way turns right to follow the path beside the railway track for about 600 m, changing sides about halfway along.

- Bear right along a series of unsigned board-walks to pick up the riverside after about 200 m. After a further 350 m down the banks, the Way crosses the River Bush by an old bridge refurbished in 1995. (This is at mile 19·9 where the beach walk rejoins the Way.)

- The path continues along the river towards the sea and reaches a large car park after 450 m. Consider a short detour of 100 m up the hill on the left to see the Lissanduff Earthworks, thought to date back to the Iron Age.

- From the car park, follow Beach Road for 650 m around a sharp left bend to the centre of Portballintrae.

North-east over Runkerry beach

5·3 Portballintrae to Portstewart

Distance	**11·4 miles 18·3 km**
Terrain	**a pleasant mixture of promenades, beaches, gravel paths and road with a brief section on grass**
Grade	**easy walking, mainly fairly flat**
Food and drink	**wide selection of places: Portballintrae, outside Dunluce Castle, Portrush and Portstewart**
Side-trips	**Dunluce Castle, The Coastal Zone, Portstewart Strand**
Summary	**mainly roadside paths to White Rocks, followed by beach walk then mainly promenades with linking clifftop paths**

20·5   1·7   4·3   3·9   1·5   31·9

Portballintrae   2·7   **Dunluce Castle**   6·9   **Portrush Harbour**   6·3   **Portstewart**   2·4   **End of Way**

- The section starts by diverting inland: in 2020 there were no signs, so follow directions closely. From Beach Road, walk west past the Bayview Hotel around the bay.

- Turn left after 100 m into a street called Dunluce Park, through a quiet housing estate. After 150 m, take the second right into Gortnee Drive.

- Go straight on to the very end of the short cul-de-sac. Turn right along the (unsigned and overgrown) narrow path behind the houses on the right.

- After 100 m, enter a field through a kissing-gate and follow the hedge on the right, gently uphill. After 200 m, pass through another kissing-gate. Head straight up for a further 100 m to reach the A2 main road.

- Turn right along the pavement beside the A2, which heads slightly uphill towards the coast. Look behind for a distant glimpse of the Chimney Tops.

Portballintrae Bay

Dunluce Castle

- After 1·4 km, the road divides to pass around a small hillock. After it rejoins, start seeing views of Dunluce Castle ahead. Turn right down a minor road at the castle sign and after 250 m reach the castle entrance on the right: see panel.

- There is an admission fee (£6 in 2020) but it's free to explore the surrounding grounds, and the 'Mermaid's Cave' below the castle.

- Resume down the minor road and turn right at the main road. After 500 m, reach a large car park at Magheracross, with great views of Dunluce Castle, White Rocks and the Skerries from its corners. This is the highest point of this stage, only about 50 m (165 ft) above sea-level.

- Continuing along the pavement, look down to the right for a series of sea arches and strangely shaped cliff faces. The one shown below is known as the Giant's Head. Above the road are tall chalk cliffs and an old quarry.

- About 1·2 km after the car park, bear right off the pavement down a path signed 'Whiterocks Cliff Path'. Descend a flight of steps, cross a footbridge and after 500 m reach a car park (with toilets). Cross over to reach Whiterocks beach with information boards.

- A detour of 100 m to the right will give you a closer view of the surreal formations in the chalk cliffs than from the road above.

- Steep sand dunes bound with marram grass provide a backdrop to Curran Strand. Out to sea are the uninhabited Skerries. *The Giant's Head*

The Arcadia café and gallery, Portrush

- Mid-way along the beach, the shore bends and the distant buildings of Portrush come into view. After a further 2½ km (1½ miles) you reach its East Strand.

- Leave the beach for a promenade that follows the shoreline, skirting the town centre. Go past the Arcadia café with play area and small inlet. Then thread your way up the steps of Bath Terrace to Bath Road and turn right down a ramp just before the Coastal Zone sign.

The Skerries

- Find out about the Coastal Zone from its website: see page 71. It is dedicated to the coastline and the National Nature Reserve of sloping rock with embedded fossils just outside.

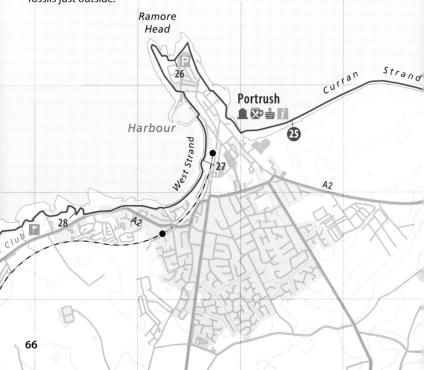

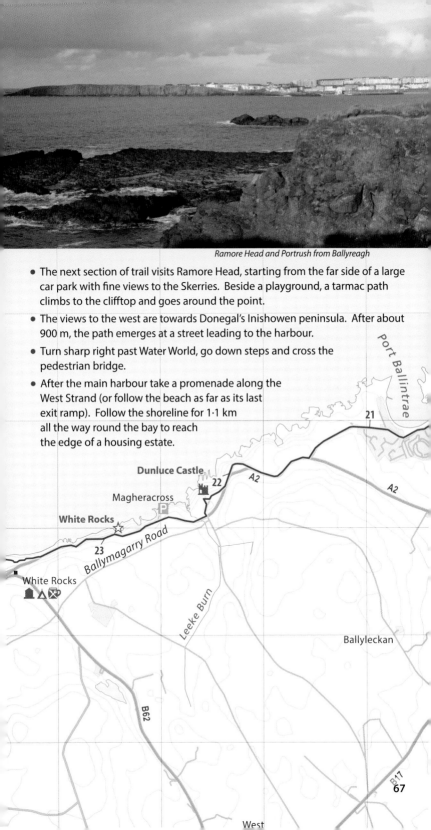

Ramore Head and Portrush from Ballyreagh

- The next section of trail visits Ramore Head, starting from the far side of a large car park with fine views to the Skerries. Beside a playground, a tarmac path climbs to the clifftop and goes around the point.

- The views to the west are towards Donegal's Inishowen peninsula. After about 900 m, the path emerges at a street leading to the harbour.

- Turn sharp right past Water World, go down steps and cross the pedestrian bridge.

- After the main harbour take a promenade along the West Strand (or follow the beach as far as its last exit ramp). Follow the shoreline for 1·1 km all the way round the bay to reach the edge of a housing estate.

Port Ballintrae

21

Dunluce Castle   22   A2

A2

Magheracross   P

White Rocks ☆

23   *Ballymagarry Road*

White Rocks

Leeke Burn

Ballyleckan

B62

B17

West

- Continue on a cycle path (NCN 93) for 400 m up to the main road. After 300 m, opposite a sign for County Londonderry, the Way turns right to resume the coastal path beside modern housing.
- A gravel path drops slightly below the level of the road and passes an inlet with a sea stack. Although very little remains, a faded information board about Ballyreagh Castle explains what stood here long ago (a tower house).
- The trail soon enters the grounds of Ballyreagh Golf Club. Cross a footbridge and turn right to descend to the shore, thus skirting the course. The path leads along secluded clifftops.
- After 600 m, it meets a lane leading to a few houses. Turn right on the seaward side of the houses to continue as signed on the route through the golf course.
- Over the next 650 m, the trail stays near the cliffs, undulating and offering the choice of a gentle or steep route, descending to pass the grave of an unknown sailor dating from the mid-1800s.
- From the cove, the trail climbs steeply to Rinagree Point and continues on past Blackrock finally to reach a restaurant Amici (former clubhouse) after 1·6 km (1 mile).
- On the far side of the car park, head up the ramp to the right to follow the blue-grey railings of the promenade past some modern apartments.
- This walkway leads to Kinora Terrace and climbs to reach Portstewart Point after 400 m. Descend the steps of Harbour Place to emerge at Portstewart's main harbour. It is manmade, designed by John Rennie and completed in 1835.
- Follow the coastline as it bends around the bay. The views ahead are towards Donegal. After 400 m, the route veers right to continue 270 m along the Crescent to the base of O'Hara's Castle (1834).
- The road leads to steps up to a well-benched walkway beside a series of coves with rocky outcrops. After 600 m, pass the old Berne salmon fisherman's cottage (dating from c1600).

Portstewart Harbour